COOL BIKES
MOTOS COOL

Connor Dayton

Traducción al español:
Eduardo Alamán

PowerKiDS press & **Editorial Buenas Letras**™

New York

Published in 2007 by The Rosen Publishing Group, Inc.
29 East 21st Street, New York, NY 10010

First Edition

Editor: Jennifer Way
Book Design: Ginny Chu
Layout Design: Kate Laczynski and Lissette González
Photo Researcher: Sam Cha

Photo Credits: Cover, pp. 1, 5, 7, 13 © Getty Images; pp. 9, 11, 15, 17, 19, 21, 23 © www.shutterstock.com.

Cataloging Data

Dayton, Connor.
  Cool bikes / Connor Dayton; traducción al español: Eduardo Alamán — 1st ed.
     p. cm. — (Motorcycles, made for speed / Motocicletas a toda velocidad)
  Includes index.
  ISBN-13: 978-1-4042-7613-0 (library binding)
  ISBN-10: 1-4042-7613-0 (library binding)
 1. Motorcycles—Juvenile literature. 2. Spanish language materials I. Title.

Manufactured in the United States of America

CONTENTS

CONTENIDO

Cool bikes can be almost any type of motorcycle. They sometimes have a **design** that has never been seen before.

Todas las motocicletas pueden ser *cool*. A veces, estas motos tienen **diseños** que no se han visto antes.

This is a new kind of motorcycle that runs on electricity. Most other motorcycles run on gas.

Éste es un nuevo tipo de moto que funciona con electricidad. La mayoría de las motos funcionan con gasolina.

Some bikes are cool because they are old. These are called **antique** bikes.

Algunas motos son *cool* porque son muy viejas. A estas motos se les llama **antigüedades**.

This small motorcycle is
called a minibike.

A esta motocicleta pequeña
se le llama mini-moto.

This motorcycle has only one wheel! It is called a monocycle.

¡Esta moto sólo tiene una rueda! A esta moto se le llama monocicleta.

Some people add finishing touches to their bikes. The owner of this bike put a furry covering on it.

Hay quienes le agregan un toque especial a sus motocicletas. Aquí, el piloto le puso una cubierta peluda a su moto.

Sometimes people give their bikes **custom** paint jobs. This bike has been painted to look like a zebra.

A veces, las personas usan pintura para **personalizar** sus motocicletas. Esta moto se pintó para parecerse a una cebra.

17

Some motorcycles are built with things that are not often used to build bikes. This bike is covered in leather!

Algunas motos usan cosas que normalmente no se encuentran en otras motocicletas. ¡Esta moto está cubierta de cuero!

19

People can add things to their bikes to make them more fun to ride. This bike has a sidecar.

Algunas personas les agregan accesorios divertidos a sus motos. Esta moto tiene un sidecar.

People also add places to store their things on their bikes. This can make taking long trips much easier.

Algunas motos tienen lugares para guardar cosas. Esto resulta muy útil durante viajes largos.

Glossary / Glosario

antique (an-TEEK) Made a long time ago.

custom (KUS-tum) Made in a certain way for a person.

design (dih-ZYN) The plan or the form of something.

electricity (ih-lek-TRIH-suh-tee) Power that makes light, heat, or movement.

---

antigüedad (la) Algo que se fabricó hace mucho tiempo.

diseño (el) El plano, o dibujo, de la forma de un objeto.

electricidad (la) Forma de energía que produce luz, calor o movimiento.

personalizar Hacer algo de manera especial para una person~